GW00701934

Introdu

Valley Press is an independent publishing house based in Scarborough, North Yorkshire, UK, bringing new fiction, non-fiction and poetry into the world – especially poetry. We've published fifty books of poetry so far, and this anthology features one poem from each.

Though still a tiny organisation, we hope to play a big part in the future of poetry publishing. If you'd like to be part of that, visit our website (www.valleypressuk.com) and sign up to the newsletter – it never descends to the level of 'spam', we like to think it's more like a letter from a friend. Give it a try!

If you're a poet yourself, you might be interested to know we are usually open for submissions of new work. Check the 'contact' page on our site for information, and keep an eye on the newsletter for more writing opportunities.

Oh, and finally – as the proud owner of this anthology, we'd like you to have 20% off any of our first fifty poetry books, when you buy through our website. Use the code **VP50** on the 'basket' page to claim that particular perk.

Thanks for reading; we hope you find much to enjoy in the following pages, and hope to hear from you soon.

Jamie McGarry,
August 2016

VP50

edited by
JAMIE MCGARRY

Valley Press

First published in 2016 by Valley Press
Woodend, The Crescent, Scarborough, YO11 2PW
www.valleypressuk.com

First edition, first printing (September 2016)

ISBN 978-1-908853-50-9
Cat. no. VP0050

Printed and bound in the EU by Pulsio, Paris.

Supported using public funding by
ARTS COUNCIL
ENGLAND

LOTTERY FUNDED

Contents

Sonnet 1

by JAMES NASH

from *Some Things Matter: 63 Sonnets* (2012)

If you should ever go, my heart would break,
Leaving a house of empty rooms behind.
If you should go, be careful what you take,
Some things matter, but others I'd not mind.
So take the books, the CDs and the fridge,
The pictures from the wall, the bathroom sink,
Take the front garden, and the laurel hedge,
For these are not important things, I think.
But leave your imprint upon the pillow,
And the faded tee-shirt you wear in bed,
Leave the battered sofa, and its hollow,
On the arm, where you always rest your head.
For if you should go, there is no doubt,
In truth, it's you I could not do without.

In Banana Warehouse

by JOHN WEDGWOOD CLARKE
from *In Between* (2014)

I met the second-hand past
of our first-hand love –
the Anglepoise, three oak chairs,
things behind things.

A Neighbour's Description

by Jonathan Davidson
from *Humfrey Coningsby* (2015)

Coningsby: landowner, of the squirearchy,
west Middle English accent, a few Welsh words.
We always took him for a strange one.
We knew he wouldn't die in his own bed,
but not either in anyone else's.
Did we ever see him with a maid? Yet,
he came back one time with the amble
of a man who'd swived and been swived
and with some words for it we didn't know.
I wasn't his friend. No one was. Once,
I lent him a small horse to take him
to the other side of the valley to see
a man about a dog. He was gone four years;
came back on foot without a word.
Still, we honoured him, you had to.

Falling

by RICHARD BARNETT
from *Seahouses* (2015)

Unforecast snow beneath my shoe, beneath snow, ice,
beneath the ice a few skeletal leaves, and then
Euston Square – though today it might be anywhere.
Is this here all the time? This world uncovered by a covering,
this world of frost-slapped surfaces and faces,
of snow-embarrassed concrete, coy and soft?

No time to ask, of course. That came and passed at four,
when salt-trucks thawed the roadways of our dreams
and each street-lamp was a snow-globe, glowing sodium.
But dawn and dream broke one another, and ice,
like time, will have its way with each of us –

The thin grey workday line of coats and boots
are living, just for now, through limbs and soles,
devoting secret, strained attention to the world
of not-quite-right angles, subtly snarled,
and gravity, governess (who teaches us
the bruised amiability of the fallen), and –

A wild, abrupt, unconscious arabesque; call it falling,
the world inverted and in a moment grasped,
my fingers reaching out through air to trace
a strange new geometry, the heart of longing and belonging,
    like falling in love.

The Grand Orrery

by Lorraine Mariner
from *Pocket Horizon* (2013)

My master's study holds the Universe
and when he has business in town
Mrs Johnson, the housekeeper, has the key

and she lets me in to wax the leather
on his desk, and dust the books that fill
the shelves, and finally I polish the planets.

There is a bronze sphere in the centre,
that's the Sun, a green and blue bauble
which is the Earth, where we live,

and next to it a pearl on a stick that looks
like a lady's hatpin – why, that's the Moon.
And there are more hatpins and more baubles

for ours is not the only Moon and not the only
World that goes around the Sun. Mr Johnson
taught me all this. He has served drinks

to the master and his friends and seen
the Orrery wound up and set in motion.
The master put a lamp in the place of the Sun

and the planets turned in their circles.
I would give my eye-teeth to see such a thing.
I told Mr Johnson I wished I was him

and Mrs Johnson said I was too much like
my star sign, the Lion, painted on the side
of that infernal contraption and she made me

stand out in the cold on the kitchen step,
which I had scrubbed that very morning,
to take a good long look at the real Moon.

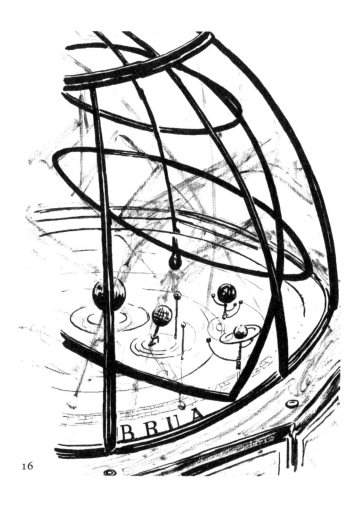

Portrait of Poet with Dimmer Switch

by Antony Dunn
from *Take This One To Bed* (2016)

Of all the home improvements he could make
he has made one – the installation of
a dimmer switch set in his writing desk
which, calibrated automatically,
maintains the light indoors a notch below
the light outside. This way he does not have
to see himself reflected in the glass
or, round him, all the things that prove him home.

This way he can address the changing of
the seasons and not once come up against
the two-faced, God-damned falsehood he's become.
The daylight hours and summer months are fine
but afternoons' and autumns' drawings-in
precurse the wastes of hours spent in the dark.

He will describe the moon and stars, the sun,
the streetlights, from his window seat, and fail
to see the one illuminating thing;
whatever light out here falls in on him.

Bed Trick

by RICHARD O'BRIEN
from *A Bloody Mess* (2014)

'Just how neurotic do you have to be
to tie a knot in a valance?' you say,
or would if you were here. I turn away,
entangled in an ersatz tourniquet
tricked up from all six beds in which we've slept –
the one we've made, and lie in, doesn't count.

And maybe our *ur*-bed exists somewhere:
a pillow that would scarcely even sink
beneath my paranoia's horse-head weight;
fluff plucked from some Platonic eiderdown.
Tucked in the folds of time, it must be there:
a duvet that could bear the space you left.

But springs replace you; finger-jab at me,
disgruntled bouncers. Restless now, I think:
the world won't let you cover all your pain
with quilt and coverlet and counterpane;
it's morning somewhere. Well, be that as it may:
sleep deeply, love, and if you can, sleep late.

The Bricklayer's Lament

by MILES SALTER
from *The Border* (2011)

The mixer span on its own orbit
the day after she left. He laid
cement on the trowel, detesting
the horizon as the wall crept up,

killing chances of junk mail
and evangelists. Anger
snapped in his wrists
as he spread the sighing glue,

inventing the wall, tall as pain.
It shrank the world, obscuring
other lives with twenty-two lines
of perfect red rectangles that said no.

He retreated, felt the border's shadow
loom against his back. The night was cool,
the rooms darker than before
as the radio hummed about hearts.

By afternoon he was itching at the quiet,
wanted a paper, a pint of milk,
chat containing eyes. Sighing, he grabbed
the hammer. A section of wall surrendered.

He stared at four bricks, saw
how they'd been tattooed from outside
with a chalky heart and arrow.
He left the house and looked for skies.

Missing the Walk at Nab Hill

by CARA BRENNAN
from *Destroyed Dresses* (2012)

Sleek men stole copper from the train tracks.
Their sly pluckings leave my carriage stranded
just outside Alnwick.

I'm late into Howarth
so watch the hills from this hotel car park;
the splendour of their height,

trace the soft outline of them,
recall your frame.
The way you stretch on your side,

defy the fierce morning. The surface of these fells
is a fine layer of hair,
your chest is covered with similar moss.

Cairns are positioned like Jenga pieces,
they cleave the wind.

Excuses Excuses

by CATHARINE BODDY
from *Lucky Dip* (2016)

He plots in the early dawn:
I can't go to school Mum.
My head aches.
I feel sick.
Don't make me go.

He rehearses as the day breaks:
I can't go to school Mum.
I've lost my P.E. kit.
I haven't done my homework.
Don't make me go.

He pleads over breakfast:
I can't go to school Mum.
My stomach hurts.
You don't understand.
Don't make me go.

As she turns away,
he whispers…
They'll be waiting for me.

Day

by PHILIPPA BLAKEY
from *A Pocketful of Windows* (2014)

This is for the mothers
whose kids weren't there when they woke this morning,
who dressed without any unusual interruptions,
whose coffee wasn't carried upstairs,
who made themselves breakfast.

This is for the mothers
who arranged their coping mechanisms
instead of flowers,
who made space on the window ledge to see the world outside
and counted their chickens, not cards.
This is for the mothers
who took the long haul down the stairs
with their third load of washing
and wondered if they would make the bottom
without an audible sob.

This is for the mothers
who didn't eat lunch,
who took some fresh air on the back doorstep
with a cup of tea and questioned
every decision they had ever made.

This is for the mothers
who were not defined by sentiment
nor bolstered by company
nor bewildered by annual exceptions
nor faced with only those faces that can be all
the questions and all the answers in every
moment of expression.

This is for the mothers
whose kids weren't there when they woke this morning
and yet
they were mothers
still.

The Crying Baby

by PETER SPAFFORD
from *Quick* (2016)

The baby was crying.

The baby was crying,
scratching his hoarse graffiti
on the clean space of the night
and his father wanted him to stop.

The books said rock him so he did.
The leaflets said hold him so he did.

He tried it all. He even tried slamming
the door of his heart shut and leaving the room
but the food he ate in the kitchen tasted of the hard bursting
sound of baby and the crying prised the door ajar.

He tried walking with the baby.
He tried driving the baby in the car.
He drove till the petrol gauge blinked
and still the baby cried, a scrawny power
jerked up bitter from the gut of the world.

He filled the car and drove to the sea,
(faced with that other unstoppable power
the baby must surely stop)
but the baby went on crying,
the baby went on crying,
the baby went on.

He took the baby to the rocks.
The waves were white dissolving snarls in the darkness
and still the baby cried.

He took the baby to the black water and lowered him.
Now the baby would sense sea and see sense and
cease.

But by the time the salt darkness should have licked
the screams and the baby away,
the tide had gone out,
there was no water.

At dawn he carried the baby to the top of the cliffs.
The seagulls giddied below him,
his belly lurched to fly,
but by the time he had let the baby like a feather into the air
(the father's body filling with a vast remembered
peace the size of space) a draught of wind had plucked
the baby up and floated him, landed him
back in his basket at home where the father found him
asleep.

More than Circumstance in Common

by Matthew Hedley Stoppard
from *A Family Behind Glass* (2013)

Shivering infant in the swimming baths
we'll have you home before long,
back to your nursery with circus wallpaper,
muffled in cellular wool.

Like a miniature Houdini, you wriggle free
of any burden on your shoulders –
unlike the nearly-man holding you afloat
in the shallow end.

Once you're reared, these mollycoddled mornings,
soothed and swaddled in honesty,
will be forgotten, but there's a double helix
that twists in both our blood;

standing up for bastards.
Midlands sinew will grip
the hands you shake, the thighs you clasp
in the bunker of adulthood.

Towelled together I feel
your delicate unfettered breath on my neck
like gale force wind through a keyhole,
an uncertain murmur, not quite a gurgle,
but the first mouthing fumble for father.

Making Silk

by JO REED
from *Stone Venus* (2011)

Only when stripped of their young are moths freed to fly;
unencumbered by the weight of their past,
they drift up to the moon,
wings disintegrating in the cold light.

Life Expectations

by NORAH HANSON
from *Under a Holderness Sky* (2013)

I expect trouble to come my way
and prepare by indulging in fearful
anticipations, my insurance cover
against the worst that can happen.
My expectations have been exceeded.

Death no longer takes me by surprise.
I am now a regular funeral-goer.
Age UK, who are expecting my death,
mail me price lists for a decent burial
I can pay for now and avoid inflation.

I wonder if they will measure me up,
allow for shrinkage of my ageing bones
and place my coffin in storage with
a sell-by date should I survive
their expected date of departure.

I expect to have morbid musings as I age.
I may become moribund like my Aunt Vera
who lay on her death bed for a whole month.
She surprised us all just before she died,
by calling out for Robert.

'Who the hell is Robert?' we asked.
Her husband Tom had died years ago
but it was Robert she called for before
taking her last breath.
Nobody expected that.

I expect to stop using dye on my hair soon.
I expect people will think me wiser when
I am white-haired, though I expect some
will disregard me or patronise me.
I expect my language will surprise them.

I expect young men who carry my suitcase
up steps from the underground will
continue to be surprised at the weight,
say 'No trouble' and make a quick getaway
before the next flight of stairs to King's Cross.

I expect the day will come when my kids
will suggest I am too old to travel on
my own and should consider selling up
and moving in with one or other of them.
I expect them not to succeed.

I expect the sun will rise each morning
whether I am here to see it or not.
I would like to be around in some form
or another, maybe in the air my
children breathe. I can't expect that –

but I can hope.

Flying Kites

by TONY HOWSON
from *The Crow Road from Eden* (2012)

I watched you in late summers,
as the heat of the days faded
and picnic baskets were packed,
deckchairs folded; modestly you
changed out of damp costumes
behind the slipping towels.

All those summers of watching
modesty grow, you furtively
watching to see who is catching
the glimpse of thigh or swelling breast;
until that summer, the one
when you refused to even undress.

All those late summers of you
running through dull light,
fading on hard sand furrows
ploughed by receding seas. Hard
on your feet through plastic sandals and
the ignored irritation of drying sand.

I watched you run, towing your kite
on a long wet string; it bounced,
cartwheeled and crashed
and crashed again, missing the breeze.
girl-stubborn, feet stomping you came
for help with another tightening tangle.

Then one summer, not the last,
the wind changed and your kite shimmered,
crackled and flew in a long, low
exciting circle of loops and swirls and
dips and dives, soaring rapidly up
before turning down with a crash – oh joy.

That summer the art came to stay
as you learnt to balance and trim
and when to tug and when to release.
Your tricks are with you, displaying
the mysteries of kite flying, on a headland
late in the summer on a breezy day.

Summer and I watched you changing,
quietly, confident in the world around you.
I watched your angled kite swooping
upwards to hang like a red kerchief
against the blue, thin cloud-lined sky,
and mine, lower, more modest in descent.

Imperfect German

by CARL POTTER
from *Form* (2012)

In my hand I hold your sepia grin,
as you sip at cold tea, talking to me
over blackened photographs of the sea;
stories of heroes, courage and gin.

In a dented jubilee biscuit tin,
love letters from old Germany.
Papier Blitz vernichtet sympathie,
covered by smiles as thin as your skin.

'*Krankenschwester Schwartz*' injects insulin.
Hakenkreuz auf foto hides beneath me.
You lie, and say that you are sleepy.
Ich bringe dich zumm bett. She tucks you in.

Du gibst einen gruß! with dirty fingers.
She lowers your hand and smiles at the pain.
You smile with your teeth, the fat nurse lingers.
Ich küsse dich tschüß and leave you again.

Sandra is a Child of Peace and Love

by HELEN BURKE
from *The Ruby Slippers* (2011)

Sandra is five foot two.
Sandra is fierce, like Boadicea.
We are on our way to Knebworth
in an old jalopy,
my red hat is floppy and
I've got sandals on
and we've got joss sticks in the van.
Joni Mitchell is playing in the park
and we've borrowed Keith's van and we're off to
Knebworth for a lark.

Sandra works at Woolies –
plastic roses, care of Daz, decorate her hair.
If you can remember Sandra in the sixties
you probably weren't there.
Me – I'm a rebel in my leopard-skin pill-box hat
and Sandra – she's a child of peace and love.

I've been selling Oz magazine in the High Street again,
I'm a student, I'm a rebel, when they call at my door –
me mam's packed me sandwiches, I said I'll be home by four.
I've got a dahlia in my hair –
if you can remember me and Sandra
you just *so* were not there –
me I'm a rebel, quintessential psychedelic,
and Sandra, she's a child of peace and love.

It's 1994, when I meet Sandra again –
she says: 'What you doing now pet?
Do you fancy a cup of tea,
we can nip down to Greggs, I've got the 40p.
Barry? The one with the headband,
he's living in Oz now –
I wish I'd never met him, what a flaming square –
as far as happiness goes, he was definitely not there.
Do you remember I was a child of peace and love?'

She says all the bairns have gone
and she's divorced twice now –
she's doing a course in self development – worra laugh –
about bloody time eh?
There are lines around her eyes,
which is no surprise to me, no not at all.
When we pass the flower seller in the Big Market,
I can almost smell that perfume of when we didn't have a care.
She says: 'Do you remember?'
I say – of course not – we were there.
I'll always be a rebel. And you are still a child of peace and love.

1969

by Paul Sutherland
from *Journeying* (2012)

Two youths, strangers on a campsite,
one Canadian, the other American,
shoot an NFL football back & forth
among shoreline pines of Michigan.
Brown polished spirals shattering
passive green. Ducking, faking, we
run patterns pro-style, knife-precise,
catching one toss at the boot straps,
even full stretch a juggling one-hander,
until every limb aching we crash down
on a spare picnic table's bench to chat.
'What' y' doin' after summer?' I ask.
— *I'm going to Vietnam. And you?*

Self Portrait with Mirror

by MALENE ENGELUND
from *The Wild Gods* (2016)

All this time,
and sleep is still Danish –
conversations guttural
as if rising from mud,
each dream coming through night
in a coat of hoarfrost,
and I wake with a word
ringing clear in the air
like the bell of Sunday.

This morning, *spejl*.
It scatters light and pictures
of childhood across the room;
snowdrifts sculpt ceiling cornices,
a midsummer fire burns
in the brass door handle,
mum's dress is a dance in the curtains.
And in the mirror,
the gaze of the girl I was;
dark and questioning, unfamiliar
with this place I've chosen as home.
I rise to greet her;
the child is weightless, lit,
a waltz of dust, she turns, and turns,
and turns and walks away.

These Bones

by Jo Brandon
from *Phobia* (2012)

It's strange to see your bones, smoke-white
and bright, know finally what you're made of;
though you took biology at school
you expect to see your heart resting mid-chest
like a set of bloody, unfeathered angel's wings,
and you think you see your soul as a shadow on the film
(because even now when you're asked to draw God
you give him a beard).
They turn the sun-box off and I am a blue-black space
'there don't seem to be any fractures'
'no breaks or splinters?' – I step up close
eager to light it up again.

Teresa's Soliloquy

by KELLEY SWAIN
from *Opera di Cera* (2014)

Each hair must be golden, or plucked.
Each pore must be purged, smoothed.

Teeth scrubbed, whitened, gleaming
with powder of arsenic. Skin gilded
with powder of saffron. Feet buffed.

'Her skin is like porcelain, her skin
is like gold.'
                This depends on light.

'Observe her swanlike neck, the curve
at her breast.'
                This depends on posture.

'Note her arching feet, her symmetrical
toes.'
                This depends on balance.

They do not feel the sweat
in the crook of my underarm.

They do not hear the purr in my belly
as lunchtime nears, and passes.

They do not know the fears
that once monthly I will burst,

a crimson flood,

and be banished at the horror
that I am not of marble made.

Danaus

by David O'Hanlon
from *History* (2016)

When my daughter played outside,
she'd carry with her round the garden,
hugged to her chest, a cracked earthen vase,
dripping water. She wouldn't let me replace it

or fix the cracks. The drops marked out
a breadcrumb trail over the decking
and the paving slabs. Never would she
reveal to me the inner secret of her game.

I'd watch from the window,
and Lucretius would muddy my thoughts:
he said *if the body's a vessel,*
then the water in it's the soul,

and each drip was time and nature
taking its toll. The price we all pay.
But I shake such nonsense away.
It's just a vase and water and a game,

a game the joy of which, as she grew older,
drained away, and now her little earthen vase
stands empty by the door,
but tries to fill with water when it rains.

Even Though You Are Where You Love

by JOANNA EZEKIEL
from *Homecoming* (2016)

and your past is a shining whirlpool
that you keep to remind yourself
of all you've left behind

some days you still hear
that voice whispering
'off you go'

and you see yourself running
just for the loose speed of it
for the pulse of your heart
that keeps up, under a clear sky

for the springy grass
beneath your feet, the tilting fence
seen from the corner of your eye

Working Title

by PATRICK LODGE

from *An Anniversary of Flight* (2013)

That Christmas,
holiday was starting;
he arrived from work on the Friday night,
defeated and defiant but still
with the odd lilt –
rolling his weight forward
on the balls of his feet,
lifting his heels
and looking upwards
beyond the wet street pavements.

Not this time walking around the long garden;
that garden he had tended
on Sunday mornings with his boys
before they were called up to Sunday roast
and its security of provision,
of sufficiency;
where the tides of money
ebbing and flowing through the house
might be stalled
until we had watched afternoon television
and slept a heavy sated sleep.

This time the front door
was opened to a knock;
he stood there,
Hector at the Scaean gates,
wanting reassurance,
offering his life of false starts;
his faith in his strength and the outside life
of men getting jobs done.

She knew at once; this had happened before
when the hard frost
made the sites resist the pick.
In Ireland, growing up, she had seen it too,
the men laid off and work not to be found;
the women a chorus of despair
flocking together and apart
looking in their common,
hard-as-flint misery
for a spark to ignite promise;
ready to work as Trojans.

In the telephone box later
I had to lie about his age,
sound as if the power lay with us;
as if there was a competition alive
to award his knowing of wood as a prize.

Digested Read

by JAMES MCLOUGHLIN
from *Encore* (2011)

The pointless comet
hurtles closer.

Its celestial lament and
commercial shadow,
an imposition on life
and yet...

I whispered to my Mother:
'What is Christmas?

What have Crocodiles or
Dundee to do with it?
Or this tree? In fact,
the planks of the concept

are ripped up, re-tiled,
gleaming, expensive, appealing.'

She began her answer:
'I know,
it's a load of bollocks.'

It's a very deep matter, actually.

How to knit a sheep

by DI SLANEY
from *Reward for Winter* (2016)

Start with the legs. It helps to
grab a hoof before casting on, or
he might kick you off. Hold the yarn
taut enough to test his strength,
loose enough to feel his flank quiver
as he bunches shanks to stretch the
ply, hoping it will fray. Loop and dip,
add sufficient stitches to keep his
interest, praise his beauty while
you unravel him, tug gently or he'll
slip your noose. Twist and roll, turn
and back again, keep your palm
against his side as you slide the pins
around about, each click a kiss,
each gartered purl a sweet low
riff to make him give it all, slough
that fleece in one soft piece
to flow from fingertips to floor.
Scoop it up and sniff warm oil
rising through his staple, the crop
he gives up now with grace. Keep
your face pressed to his curls,
breathe the heat and wax of him
behind his ears as hands move
faster as you near the end, his chest
bare and cold, your feet hot under
so much weight. Tie the ends off tight
before you let him go, your nose to his
in thanks only eskimos understand.

Ripper

by Daniela Nunnari
from *Red Tree* (2012)

He brings me wild things,
wild things with wings.
He leaps into the still and silent sky
to murder my metaphors.

He holds them in his mouth a while,
then lays them out before me on the floor.
Death is his gift.

Yet still I hope for the things with feathers.
Still I cradle them. Their tiny hearts beat rhythms in my hand.
Still I carry them outside, and stroke their heads and place
    them on the ground.

With whispered apologies I retreat,
to watch them from the window,
to pray they'll fly away.
Sometimes they do.

Sometimes we bury them.
As cold and stiff as cardboard boxes.
Crosses made from twigs pushed into soil
beneath the bushes they were born in.

And I scream at him and scold him,
lock him in and shut him out,
no longer welcome on my knee, my bed,
his head pushed in my palm.

And I hate him but I love him though I hate what he has done.
And before too long he's back beside me, his face against my own.
And I forgive and he forgets
and balance is restored.

Then he brings me things,
wild things with wings,
and lays them on the floor.

A Rumor of Birds

by Saleem Peeradina
from *Final Cut* (2016)

In my sleep, birds stream silently overhead – flocks of them –
wave after wave of a high altitude river unbound
by banks, wings riding the wind, navigating by stars in the pitch
black of night, or the water's magnetic glaze.
Sometimes, they storm above my roof in a cloudburst
of feathers, squawks, and screams.

One watching through a telescope will see them
scatter like flakes of pepper against lunar light.
but mostly, these night-travelers will pass invisibly, afloat
on a murmur. Before daybreak, they sift down
to settle in the trees or fields to awaken us with their
morning songs. After dusk, they flutter up again to migrate south.

Jays, thrushes, blackbirds, finches, wrens, larks, swallows, tanagers,
warblers, orioles – you live, love, breed, and die at full tilt
claiming only a bit of earth and infinite sky.

Voice, cry, call

by Adam Strickson
from *Wingbeats* (2012)

Imagine if they invaded Leeds in March,
made The Headrow their cliff face,
cemented nests on every ledge –
how you'd never hear yourself speak
above their din, truckloads of sound
emptied out on every corner.

Crackled bicker of shriek –
kitt-ee-wake, kitt-ee-wake, kitt-ee-wake –
every car alarm in the multi-storey
triggered, echoing the concrete floors
while the flocks scrawl KITTS RULE
in guano on every wall and lift door.

You'd soon become desperate for August
when the thousands would take off,
cross the ring road and cooling towers,
head off over the Wolds to the coast,
fly over a lad in a wetsuit who teeters
on a ledge at Flamborough Head.

They'd head out to the North Sea,
beat off the slap of rough storm.
They'd scrape their un-rosined bows
across the growl and snarl of waves
while we cleaned the stink from the city
and learned to talk human again.

Voyeurs

by DAVID AGNEW
from *There Are No Such Things As Seagulls* (2012)

I discovered two seagulls
staring in the window
as I stood naked
drying off after a shower.

I did not think
they were impressed,

but
they turned up
the next day
for another look.

Beach chalets

by JOHN WEDGWOOD CLARKE
from *Sea Swim* (2012)

are small wooden stanzas
in which words undress
and step from the damp
boards and sixty-watt bulbs
into colossal light,
blinking, rubbing arms,
lifting a little on their toes
as if trying to see over the cold,

ready as they will never be
for the body to speak itself again
for the first time
in the mouth of the North Sea,
the body like a bell note
struck by an iron key,
wordless in a furl of murk,
weed, someone's foot,

and up, shouting, turnstones
overhead, the Hispaniola
rocking by, treading water
back into now, rooted
in all the strange words
– children, parents –
in hands that have held
and let go, swimmers in song.

Bath Poem

by Rowena Knight
from *All the Footprints I Left Were Red* (2016)

She spends an indecent amount of time in the bath
emerging only to write poems
about being in the bath.

When her fingers turn to soft walnuts
she knows it is time to press them to the keyboard.
She has determined the ratio of water to word.

There is always bubble bath, of course.
She writes of how it pearls her breasts.
She might even mention the dark triangle of her "sex".

Her poems don't mention the mould
congregating in ceiling corners.
She never slits a swatch from her knee whilst shaving.

She is committed to the art of the bath poem:
always naked, always clean,
waiting for you like a peach.

Billy Bragg's Beard

by KATE FOX
from *Jagger's Yurt* (2013)

Billy Bragg's beard bristles at inequality,
has got fascism by the short and curlies.
Billy Bragg's beard is not red but it should be.
It is strongest on the far left.
Well-travelled whiskers
which don't believe in stopping close shaves and rash moments.
Billy Bragg's beard is all about active growth and change;
shows that a small group of committed hairs
can change the face of man.
Billy Bragg's beard has been accused of going country,
owes a debt to Woody Guthrie.
Billy Bragg's beard will frame direct words until justice wins
and (he says) hides a multitude of chins.

Forget what you've been told

by JO BRANDON
from *The Learned Goose* (2015)

The kindliest fallacy
is that you should always keep things simple.
Say what's in your heart!
But romance is a craft;
the reason we sparked fire,
spat words
and searched for obscene metaphor
in dull places.

Tell me, do you want to be a lover?
Are you ever excited by shopping lists,
or the prospect of writing thank you cards
for hoards of wedding gifts?
No, because you've been told
that love is mishap and adventure.
I offer up the true fundamentals:

Lesson one: you must accept
all true love is cut short –
there will never be sufficient years.
Time refuses to expand
so you must make room in your chest.

Lesson two: real love is painful,
a cigarette butt to the heart.
Any loss of love will burn right through you.

Lesson three: love does not equal happiness.
Happiness apes love,
it is a new-fangled measure of longevity.
If love always equates to happiness
I'm afraid you're still
doing it all wrong.

Gooseberry

by James Nash
from *Cinema Stories* (2015)

They ask me to go to the cinema with them,
and I go, touched that as a couple
they are prepared to share.

I sit with them,
all of us munching and chatting,
not feeling at all like a gooseberry
until the film starts
and they somehow get closer,
and while they are watching
occasionally touch each other on the leg.

It looks nice, friendly even;
I consider for a moment just joining in,
putting my hand on one of their knees,
but stop myself just in time.
Then I look at the legs of strangers down the row
and wonder whether they would like it.
It could be a bit of an ice-breaker.

But I rein myself in;
and instead touch one of my own legs,
and rub it lightly in a clockwise direction.
It feels surprisingly good;
but just in case anyone is looking,
I pat my leg fiercely
and stamp my foot down hard
as if I've got
pins and needles.

Sleeping Child

by John Wedgwood Clarke
from *Ghost Pot* (2013)

You sleep, while names of villages rise
and fall away, tail-lights dwindling ahead
until only we summon the sign
for crossing deer, steer by the constellation
of a pub. The edges where the wipers
shove the rain gel and tremble, sucked thin
by small riptides. I rest my elbow on
the door-frame like my father would and read
the road through fingertips. A milestone
unfolds, lets go of the verge, the barn owl
gone before I realise – that's how we get home.
And what will you recall of the sudden lift
from car to bed, your eyes broken open
for a moment by the light in the hall?

The Light of You

by NORAH HANSON
from *Love Letters and Children's Drawings* (2011)

In the dreamtime before waking,
I lived again a winter afternoon
alone with you; the light fading
from the window, a coal fire,
the smell of baking bread,
the child I was listening as you
sang to music playing on the radio.

You twirled and clapped your hands.
I sat on the kitchen floor, flexing
my toes to the rhythm of your dance.
When the music stopped, my infant
voice called you to squat beside me.

Your smile crinkled lines round your eyes.
The light of you touched me.
I had no words to tell you this.

You stroked my hair, touched your lips
to my head. I butted into your warmth,
nuzzled into the smell of you.
You lifted me. Desire made me whimper
until my mouth filled with the flesh of you.
You wiped away my dribble.

Today you move your hand to the rhythm
of my voice singing the songs of your youth.
I stroke your hair, touch my lips to your head.
You whimper your need. I hold a drinking cup
to your mouth and wipe away your dribble.

Your smile crinkles lines round your eyes.
The light of you touches me.
I tell you this.

The Poetry Stall

by MARK WADDELL
from *On the Cusp of Greatness* (2016)

I'd sat there
all week

not a man
woman
or
child
stopping to have a look
at my wares

the hand-painted sign
swinging gently in the breeze:

poems to order

as I was packing up for the day
a small dog
nuzzled my leg
and
I wrote a note:

give this dog a bone

and placed it along with a few coins
in a worn leather bag around the animal's neck
nudging it towards the butchers.

we have
been doing this together
for a long
and
very
happy
time.

Baxter's Crime

by Helen Burke
from *Here's Looking at You Kid* (2014)

Baxter, the dog, is being dragged down the lane.
Again.
I feel sorry for Baxter, in fact, most days –
I feel a bit like him.
Pulled this way and that.
Someone behind me with a lead that I can't see.
Baxter has no idea what his crime is.
(Nor have I.)
Just that he is a dog who takes his time, perhaps.
He investigates. Sniffs too long in all the wrong places.
I can never hear the words – just that she is shouting,
snapping and snarling.
I imagine the teeth are bared – the hackles grizzly and raised.
But Baxter I feel is undeterred.
He will go on being Baxter.
He will go on going on.

There is no cure for being free of mind and will.
Baxter, my friend, my alter ego.
Baxter – I love you.
Go on being, Baxter.

(Run amok – remain a dog with pluck.)

You bark at your side of the wall
and I will bark at mine.

Yiannis in His Bar

by PATRICK LODGE
from *Shenanigans* (2016)

Yiannis in his bar is restless; counting covers,
cradling a cappuccino, he watches

the impossibly taut, tanned staff make money
for him in accents from the Steppes.

He stares at a waitress's legs, remembers wild
nights, drinking with cockney spivs,

dancing film-star syrtaki with peroxide women;
flips worry beads like an impatient groom.

Yiannis lights up his one for the night; rests, where
old men have smoothed the pebble seat

shiny as an ossuary. Eclectic House from his bar,
soundtracks the mute satellite football;

Yiannis conjures the punch of rock 'n' roll, the smell
of patchouli and lust in the backstreets.

Bells toll from the Panagia; incense coils from a censer,
the choir chant the *Kontakion of the Dead*:

Yiannis recalls village girls in their innocence,
forsees his spotless wine-washed bones.

He spits and flicks his butt into the churchyard:
neither sickness, nor sorrow, nor sighing.

You and Me

by Michael Stewart
from *Couples* (2013)

You eat an apple an orange and a banana every morning.
I drink a bottle of red and four pints of stout every evening.
You only drink water from Sainte-Catherine spring.
I only drink water if I've just been sick.

You eat wheat germ and linseed and organic cranberries.
I eat lime pickle and fried egg sandwiches.
You say your angel is enshrined in light,
your angel guides you to your Pilates.

My angel only comes out at night.
He whispers that I'm ill, mad and dying.
You wrote 'I love you' with sugar on the kitchen tiles.
I spilt salt in the goldfish bowl and then lied.

You never drink and drive.
I always have the requisite two pints.
You go your way and I'll go mine
and we will meet at the end of time.

A Train and a Fox

by Oz Hardwick
from *The Ringmaster's Apprentice* (2014)

This is not Adlestrop – you'd be hard pressed
to romanticise this unscheduled stop by York
Sewage Treatment Works. The scent of grubby grass
is overpowered by a chemical stench
worse than the stink it masks.

The Class 144 Pacer fails
to add that touch of nostalgic steam –
it's simply inconvenient at the end
of a long day. There are no announcements
as 'customers' fidget and hiss into mobiles.

Then, from out of the scrub by the grey fence –
a fox. Make no mistake, he is not Reynard
or Chaucer's Daun Russell. At best
he is *vulpes vulpes*, but won't answer to that either,
nor will he escape the gallows, nor even talk.

No, as a living, breathing fox, he will not consider
narrative, metaphor, or abstract symbol. Yet,
before resuming his animal business, our eyes meet
and, between a bland train and an unconcerned fox,
hangs more poetry than I will ever write.

The Minutes

by MILES SALTER
from *Animals* (2013)

In the morning fresh minutes are waiting.
Hundreds crowd your bed, litter the floor.
There are so many, threading

down the stairs and out the door.
In the evening, as the sky darkens,
you look for the minutes but most

have gone. As you watch, another
vanishes. The phone rings.
Two minutes go.

In bed, you close your eyes
and ask for more.

Bearing Gifts

by DAVID HUGHES
from *Ex Libris* (2015)

I am driving west for Christmas,
towards the M40, Oxford ahead of me.
In my mirror a full moon hangs
low over London, and the radio
murmurs on without distraction

except for the News. Poland
has Military Rulers, and Christmas,
foodless under steady snow,
is in doubt. There is rioting
in Gdansk, and in Katowice small groups

resist the Militia hopelessly;
but I am untouched until at Uxbridge
I pass the eagled column, for Polish airmen
forty years ago defending us. Overhead
white contrails drift in blue September skies

while I think eastwards where others alone
or in convoy travel bearing gifts.
The sun clouds, then sets; and my headlamps
light on flakes suddenly rising in the arc
of wipers. I queue at every junction.

Communion Anthem

by Nigel Gerrans
from *It Is I Who Speak: Selected Poems* (2015)

This is my body, offered you,
A body, torn and racked with pain,
Calling you back to walk my way,
And know your finer selves again.

This is my life-blood harshly shed,
Drained to the last for care of you,
Calling you from the vain and false,
To claim the beautiful and true.

I had no other I could share,
There was no more that I could give,
Open your hands at my table here,
Come, that you may learn to live.

My feast shall fill you with my life,
My love shall hold you day by day,
You are to be my body now,
So dare to give yourselves away.

Bearing Witness

by FELIX HODCROFT
from *Life After Life After Death* (2010)

Launching our paper planes
down the stairwell
into darkness.

Taking a walk
when you've been sick
(or remember you're dying).
It's spring and
the birdsong the tight buds the breeze the taste
of start again swallow and smile.

Glimpsing the silver spokes hurtling past
to leave you behind.
Sticking your grainy walking-stick into 'em.
Oh calamity!

The ground is full of the young and unwilling
who nevertheless had to pass.
We tread on their heads every day.
Much worse to betray them
by time-wasting.

The sun slips round the manor house
like an assassin.
The morning-room windows are
cold now.

Skimming stones over the deep mere.
Truth-telling.

Working at happiness
like a master-carpenter who
turns a block to
a delicate, intricate carved toy
a child can love
and pass on
          and pass on
                    and pass on.

Waiting. Watching. Listening.
Then launching our paper planes
down the stairwell and
into darkness.

The Poet Knocked

by ROBERT POWELL
from *All* (2015)

The poet knocked on my door
as I sat dreaming at my desk
in that summer of hesitation
while the heron landed the dusk.

The desk was made from a door
which was open and shut forever
and in case of heartbreak or fire
would fly to the river, where

another place would be waiting,
a house that was safe for the heart,
a heart-house safe, save
for the risk of drowning

in dreams that could turn
from cliché to danger,
like certain words
and the lives lived near them.

> *I have things to say*
> *that I know you've forgotten,*
> *I have her address*
> *and the map to her heart,*
> *I know the way*
> *to the path to your joy,*
> *and all you could be*
> *if only you started;*

the road through the forest,
the place of the key,
the way you can make
the locked lands free

He knocked again
and he knocked again.
As though stood behind him,
out there in the garden,

I could see him hammer:
that small, tense shape
of sad, fierce hunger
at the locked red door.

I didn't answer,
sat still and waited.
The heron and the summer flew
and only now do I know what I knew.

The New Dress

by Jo Reed
from *Life Class* (2015)

In this dress I will abseil down Everest,
tread my tightrope with a new dexterity
above the Tyne, spin on a pin with angels
amazed in the nave of Beverley Minster.

In this dress I'll dance down red carpets
without leaving marks, face down the dog
barking black through night's blanket,
then pillow my head in unbroken sleep.

In this dress, with promises I can keep,
I'll lob secret messages all over the net,
deal daily with Talk Talk, and other things
sinister, eat caviar for breakfast, place bets

on that missing Minister of State, wassail
with a choir on the deck of Invincible
as she flags sad goodbyes, ship to shore;
eat oysters on Fridays, *always* ask for more.

I will finish poems, win prizes galore,
ignore the front cover of *Grazia*, where
they have a portrait of me – in *this dress* –
holding the Oscar for 'Best Screenplay'.

In this dress, I'll buy an old printing press,
wing-walk my Cessna on the way to Venice,
eat fritto misto overlooking the sea,
bombard men with trifle whenever I please.

Invitation

by Mike Di Placido
from *A Sixty-Watt Las Vegas* (2013)

One day
it *will* happen –
that Italian feast in the garden:

long tables
under pergolas
clustered with grapes;

pasta, vino, dancing
and music – oh yes – definitely music;
Gigli, Pavarotti *and* Sinatra, capisce?

But most importantly, on the guest list, you.

And when the stragglers
are laughing down the lane
to their taxis and cars,

we'll sit
by the little gnarled apple tree,
as thudding moths shake the lanterns,

and I'll thank you, then,
with the backing of the open heavens
until the dying of the last star.